Poetry is Blessed by God

Catherine C. Inserra

A publication of

Eber & Wein Publishing
Pennsylvania

Poetry Is Blessed by God

Copyright © 2025 by Catherine C. Inserra

All rights reserved under the International and Pan-American copyright conventions. No part of this book may be reproduced, stored in a retrieval system, or transmitted in any form, electronic, mechanical, or by other means, without written permission of the author.

Library of Congress
Cataloging in Publication Data

ISBN 978-1-60880-790-1

Proudly manufactured in the United States of America by

Eber & Wein Publishing

Pennsylvania

Poetry Is Blessed by God

The Truck, Brown House, and Paradise Farm

I, Peter Tasso, went to work in the morning, passed brown house, with mother Emily and darling daughter name Lisa Susan.

I love Lisa Susan; she had sating hair, and she was always by the window. There was my work paradise farm a few miles away. Work was a lovely scene. Birds of blue sapphire, red, and yellow roses, a salute to spring, and music filled the clouds. I took Lisa one night out to dinner and felt deeply in love. We got married and lived in a brown house.

Time passed, and we died each other arms. Light appeared outside the mansion and the heavenly gates opened. We were amazed how beautiful the diamond Heaven was.

Then we rode the sky stairs to our new apartment. In the mist outside the house skull was crying because he will never see the light fantastic. He loved no one in life; deeper he went into the crept underworld of the rain clouds.

In Heaven with God Life Was Armful of Love

In Heaven, the world is more beautiful than Barth sky. It is a blessed blue that warms the soul and body. The soul is art and paintings of saints and Jesus Christ. Everyone doing their chores like renewing all arts and singing a new song, or God creating something for His heavenly family. God makes them clothes like robes with saber stripes or golden stripes. He listens to their prayers for a peaceful United States, so there be peace on Earth.

He listen to His angels and people who live with God. The people of Heaven pray for us, unite with us, and with us last romance and happiness. God loves poetry and His flowers make Him happy. Poetry is a music to the magic of the sky blue perfume that twinkle stars and moon and planets.

Teaching the Animals Like Dogs and Cats

I have to say, I have plans after death. As soon as I die, I want to do God's deal. I want to tell God I want to be a teacher. My name is Frances. I like to go into their lovely world and teach them to talk. I want to be useful in Heaven. There is a future for dogs and cats. Some of the animals who come into this world again be intelligent, talk, and can tell us if they are sick and maybe some dogs will be teachers. In the past they were treated exactly from now on, they will be classified and praised for their ability to do good things.

For that, I will be happy. I made them smart to help people and older folks. God was wonderful to make them and give them right to blessed the dogs to love man and God to make dogs.

In Marriage There Must Be Good Intention and to Be In Love

Women need man to give them strength, knowledge, and happiness.

A woman should walk down the earth knowing she will be good, honor her husband, and obey the Ten Commandments. She should love her children more than herself. She should ask God to give her wisdom and grace, walking in the path of beauty and cherishing her husband and children. She should teach her children to love God and people.

Respect older and try to help unfortunate people of the world. Every child has a right to get medical care, food, and shelter. Everyone should love their children and pray for other children that love conquers all and love will brighten you years. Please bend down and love one another passionately until the end of time.

A Doman Who Jesus About Bange Alter

Into the night, Luis Caraj dreams about dancing in Paris.
It is evening and it is dark, and silvery silk is flowing into the air.
Her beautiful silver bell shoes shine in the mist of the clouds.
She's doing her basic steps and feels so confident she is dancing on the stairs of the sky.
Starts trembling all around her, saying Lisi, you will be a brilliant star someday. Be patient and study hard, you are so loved by everyone. Dance the night away sparkling the dark mystic of good talent.

My Beautiful Portrait I Love So Much

Into the picture of life I steer and there is a beautiful woman. It is my mother of sating dark hair, rosy cheeks, and clear complexion. She is so beautiful. There is never being a woman so radiant on the floor; she was also beautiful inside, caring about others and helping others in need. She loved her husband and worshipped her daughter. She died a long time ago.

I cannot forget her lovely smile or good thoughts of wishes. She was love so much by relatives and friends. Sometimes the woman reminds me of a saint. Being in Heaven, how she must be more beautiful and desirable. She will pray for your happiness. Somewhere there is a beautiful portrait smiling down on your soul.

Dracula Who Tried to Hurt a Nice Lady and Kind Soul

Dracula's name was Red Collins, who was cursed by a witch named Carl Kings. She hated Red because he did not trust her and wanted her to leave him alone. Dracula loved a girl name Rachel. Rachel could not stand him. Rachel wondered why he was always seeing at night. Always wearing black clothing. He did not want to bite Rachel, but Red Collins was getting sick over his snob ways. One night he craved her blood and killed Carol King because he needed blood. The next day, Rachel found Carol King dead. The police had a hard job to find her. Rachel told the police to check on Red Collins, only one round at night. Police entered his estate; one morning entered the Dracula home they found him in a coffin. The police put a stab to his heart and he perished, flew like a bird in a sky. Rachel was happy he died and married her boyfriend Vincent Cielo. She was happy and safe again. May Red Collins never come back.

Cinderella Dock Married the Prince of Dockers

There was a princess name Cinderella, pretty, blonde who lived in a lovely castle of Spain. Her favorite color was yellow. She loved John Smith, a prince of Hell.

The prince would rise at night from Hell to see Cinderella. Dark prince was sweet; he did not tell Cinderella where he really came from.

He kept on dating Cinderella; she finally fell in love with him. John was smart; he did not tell the princess the truth. He wanted her soul in Hell.

So they started to plan their wedding and did not know where he wanted to live. Cinderella should have been more wise before she agreed to this marriage.

So the night turned into day, Cinderella trying her wedding dress on, yet she looked lovely, but she did not know why she felt sad. She began to have nightmares and bad dreams. The next day Cinderella ignored her dreams and planned the royal wedding. John Smith said let's not wait. But Cinderella said I want to be sure. Cinderella wanted to be married in September, John Smith was mad, he wanted to control Cinderella. Finally Cinderella did not want to marry Smith. She felt in love with Captain Koob and Cinderella Koob was finally happy. John Smith went back to hell and danced the night in dust and his vampires.

Another World Found Live with a Stranger from Another Planet

There was an old woman, her name was Sandra Field, she was older than 88. Sandra never found life on Earth and accepted her faith. Then from planet time, wanted to grab another Earth to have someone he could live.

He saw looking into a safe woman, Sandra Field. He decided to pick her up. James Tredion went to ring at her apartment and Sandra opened her door. She said, you the one who called me? She asked him where he lived, Sandra far away in Toms River. I live in Washington, DC. So they went to the movies, then dancing, they stayed awake, then he took her home to rest.

Someday I will tell you where I come from, Sandra, until then. They kept seeing each other and enjoying their relation. Then it came one night when the stars were shining, two people falling in love. He told Sandra the truth that he was from another planet. In time, he wanted to marry Sandra, in time to live in his time R galaxy. They bought a great time R galaxy and lived happy.

But when they reach time R God made them both young and they were in love. Dreams do come true when two souls found each other.

The Sailor Boy

One day, there was a sailor boy. He had a white Nifora, he loved ships and liked his job on another sailor's boat. He cleaned the decks and loved his work every day. Sometimes he got off the boat and went to the towers. He stopped at a bar had a few drinks. He saw young women in the bar. Frankie was shy and didn't want to associate with them. He went back to the ship and had his dinner. The next day he got impressed, by topping to other port, and enjoyed his day. Then he reached again the ship docked in San Francisco and went to a bar where he met a girl who also was shy and did not want to go out with him. He sent home to the ship. He did not want to go to another bar, so he decided to stay on the ship. One day the ship gave a party for all the sailors. Nice girls were invited, and one girl liked Frankie and started to date Frankie.

Frankie was happy and liked Jade, soon after that the couple got married and a couple of months Frankie was to leave the Navy. They got an apartment and were very happy.

Always wait for the right girl and trust always the right girl. Old sailor boy Frankie was a happy old soul. Never to be sad again.

The Song of Happiness Is Misa

I love to sing, I love to see the mountains on Garrett Mountains. The mountains are purple majesty and the grass as poet heart. Sky is a light blue color; my soul was gage with the world.

I walked up to the top of the mountains. I felt like the king of France with forty thousand man I felt I should inspire a little song. I sang, I felt the sky, mountains there stand tall how was flowing she scared me and climb to the top with the king from its queen. She helped him create a song in honor of the purple mountains.

The queen said, let us inspired mountains, belong to us in our hearts, they live in our soul. We are inspired by love and always will be faithful in our religion. Souls combine and we will reach Heaven higher than the magical mountains.

Children Hopes

I see a child cry, and love it. I see hope and crisis. Children need food, care and love. World help children when you give to help poor children give with your heart.

Children need clothing and food and to be loved. Everyone needs divine help, especially children all over this world. It hurts them not to eat; they must be strong to go to school.

Love those babies; give them the gift of hope. Without help, they will die. They need someone to bread their hearts and give what they can. Someday the world will change and all children will be helped and guided. Children are a gift of Heaven. Let's all pray and give to the church tools that will arise to strong human being. Feed their body, warm their souls. Put love in their hearts so children will grow up as good citizens and happy people will arise with a song of life.

Love Conquers

I hear singing and my soul is happy. I feel dancing and my heart is on fire. Love is a wonderful thing. Love is the coming of a better future. Love is lovely and best of great news. A young bride's lovely romance. Hollywood is on fire with great talents. New actors new songs of glamour's stars-famous actress like Debbie Reynolds who sang "Singing in the Rain."

There is a lot of talent in Hollywood. The actors work hard to give you happiness in hopeful situation. The music box was startling in the beginning and now in the future it promotes greatness. Films will be more brilliant and the industry will be perfect. The industry will climb to the high sky of America. Life won't be dull; movies will make the earth lovelier than ever.

In Heaven People Will Be Treated Like Prince and Princess

In Heaven, it is such a beautiful palace. God the Father is truly a good Father. He will be sure we have niece pieces of jewelry, shiny shoe of red leather. We will be able to eat. We will wear robes of the finest linen. Our ears with golden earrings. Our heads will be crowned with precious diamonds made by God's hands. We will go to school and education will continue. Heaven will be sparkling with gold flowing curtains and precious stones, never found on Earth and in another planet. Animals will be treated kindly and loved by God. No greed or lust, no fighting, no killing. Person will live in music and poetry, all will be happy and love and respect each other.

Poetry is the talent that God gives us; in poetry there is true spirit. Only in Heaven wishes and birthdays come true.

God Helps Rita Rose

There was a girl named Rita Rose. She was a nice girl and attended St. Peter's church. Rita was married with a daughter name Gloria. She was a good daughter and joy to her mother's heart. Rita worked hard and had no husband. Her husband died of cancer. Rita had to raise Gloria Rose. Gloria helped in the house when her mother worked at Valley Hospital. In the hospital, Rita worked as a dishwasher and had four floors of dishwashing duty. They paid Rita well and she was a hard worker. Gloria made the best at home and cleaned dishes and floors.

Rita Rose started to feel tired and sickly, so she went home to pray to God for help. One night Rita went home and an angel opened the door for her. Gloria was sleeping in the other room and the angel had a cup with blood made by God.

It was Jesus Christ Son of God. Jesus told Rita to drink the cup of blood. The next day Rita felt strong again, she was cured by the Lord's blood. Her story is to state that everything is possible for God.

Dracula Who Tried to Hurt Someone Nice

Dracula's name was Red Collins, who was cursed by witch named Carol King. Carol hated Red because he did not trust her and wanted her to leave him alone. Dracula loved a girl name Rachel Fry. She could not stand him. Rachel wondered why he was absent in the day, and always wearing black clothing. Red Collins did not want to bite her but Red Collins was getting sick over her moreish ways. One night he craved blood and killed Carol King. The next day Rachel found Carol King dead. The police had a hard job to find clues. Rachel told police to check on Red Collins, only seen at night. The police entered his estate the Dracula Inn. Police found him in a black coffin, put a stick thru his heart and he perished like a brief in the sky. Rachel was happy he died and married her boyfriend Vincent Cielo. She felt safe.

May Red Collins never come back, no one pull out the thick stick in his heart. Beware!

Be My Love, Let Us Raise and Shine in Harmony

    Be my love Ruth, so princes and kind to me and always honor thee. I love your silvery hair, your golden smile, your beautiful soul that fills my being. Love is in the air, the sky in your lips, your heart beats for me dearest. I love your palms with starving heart. I'll never let you go. If possible in the death to Ruth as I study your face, with such tenderness. I feel like climbing the tree to the sky. Overwhelmed by Love's sweet serenade, you are my life, you are my world, you are my reason to be alive.

Paul, I never want to let you down and never let you go. You are my breath of love. I can feel your heart beating when our eyes meet. God never let me and Paul stop loving each other. We tried to take love serious because it's the best of life. Without love and romance, life would end. Life will be empty and the air will not have the odor of perfume.

God Bless Our Congressman for Senate

God bless all our congressmen for senate. God bless our lawmakers; they make law to protect our people. We the people of the United States.

We must respect their laws even if we do not understand them. The laws protect our country, its people, its government, our family and friends, and the justice of the world.

The blessed virgin loves the United States of America. We must pray to her, the queen of Heaven. Earth could be beautiful if we prayed to God. God the Supreme Being perfect, who made all things. Keep them in existence. The love of Lord and the persons who make our outstanding love and our wonderful United States, a government to be proud of and admire. Come on hanging our flags high in the sky to touch the Heaven and glory be to our nation and we the people.

I Was a Little Girl, I Love to Watch Betty Grable in Christmas

I lost my mother when I was ten years old. I loved to go to the movies and watch Betty Grable. Now I like to watch all pictures, her dancing, and beautiful singing.

It made me happy to see her because I thought of her as a mother. She played in pictures, like I wake up screaming with friend Victor Martinez and mother.

Now I am old and I feel warm to see her pictures; they still make me happy and my heart warm, too.

I wish we could live forever so we do not miss our loved ones. I hope to see her in the next world. I pray she likes me. Maybe love means more in the next world.

Movie stars work hard and deserve to be remembered. Don't you agree with my poetic friends and loving nature?

Dreams of Love

Dream away, my love, unto a special character young and a world to conquer and be mystified. Dreams of bringing desire that set my soul on a journey of dying amber. An amber so sweet it thrills me sphere. Holding you in my arms, fast breath taking love to hold you herself fairy dust. Your body so sculpture and confusing. I want you to touch my burning help of retune sense.

Down and down the mountains we go our bodies like Humpty Dumpty in love.

Serenade with the sense of breathing, fired wind, and a blast of all captain off the ocean wind.

Come to me I would hold you so tenderly as a trophy for our enemy conquered love.

Let's dance to the moon already we bring the mountains. Set aside our desire for the moon will bounce us to the end of requiring time. None to cease these for angels trait life conquer souls and destiny will flow forever.

Earth Is in Trouble Since the Beginning of Time

Earth has fallen into destruction: Does it matter if the earth is destroyed? Earth has fallen down since the time of Adam and Eve. When they disobeyed God and were living out of the Garden of Paradise. When Moses gave the Ten Commandments. Moses the ten commandments out mountains, replacing themselves with evil, lust, and greed.

When Noah had to build an ark to save Noah and his people. When the emperor of Rome bans Rome because a lot of deaths. Innocent people were killed and sweet babies died. At that time the devil was over and over, and there was starvation for this hellish act. We must live on a healthy planet. When lives are safe and in good care, rich man don't care about the poor men, especially terrorists, who called and destroyed on 9/11 thousands of people destroyed and perished and the relatives of 9/11 were hurt because they loved their relatives and everyone there.

The Artist Who Came Alive at Midnight at the Art Gallery

In the dark of the night, a beautiful lady called Connie hanged on the gallery walls. Connie was indeed a mission of life. Everyone who came to the gallery looked at her picture; she was beyond a mystery.

One lady said, "I say her eyes moved. Her brown eyes sparkle like diamonds. A smooth, lovely face like starlight's and blowing glow to her blond hair.

One night, Martha saw a bright light of mist come out of the canvas. She came out of the frame and wanted to live and be a real lady. I said to myself maybe God put another soul in Connie and she came to life. Connie will be happy and have a chance to thank God for this miracle. Myself is always in flights and the artist who created Connie, will passed her on the street wondering why she seem so familiar.

Girl Who Almost Lost Her Life from Appendix

My name is Margaret Sielo. I live in the Bronx, New York City, with father and mother. I Margaret started to get pains on my right side of the belly. My mother was Phyllis Sielo; she took me to the doctor. The doctor said I needed to take my appendix out. My mother refused; she thought I was too young for this operation. My father John thought I should have surgery and be safe.

I insisted two weeks that I got sick and ran a high fever. My mother Phyllis called the doctor Vincent Caprio who came to the house. He told my mother I was dying and could not help me. My mother had tears in her eyes and called another doctor who came to the house. My mother felt strong and trusted God. The doctor was Rubino. He told my mother to put ice packs on my right side and by some mysterious reason, I felt better and wanted something to eat. My mother had a priest in the house and called him to my bed side. He told everyone to bend down and pray to God. Everyone was on their knees and said prayers to God. The priest told everyone that God worked a miracle in this house. My appendix fell asleep for 30 years in my stomach, when Dr. Todd in Ridgewood, New Jersey, took it out thirty years later.

Breathing Eyes of Gold

Into the mist of an enchanting planet is a breathing eye of God. Ah! It is the sudden beauty that the eyes can tell, so beautiful with liquid gold. Eyes shined like gold masterpiece.

Into the eyes shines, crying of such honorable love. Its beauty of God's soul, intelligence, and powerful foreseen. He existed through a planet of all God's doing. He is planet destined all, the powerful God. One God existed then God of the Garden of Eden, Adam and Eve should bad ideas and should listen to God.

Now God created a new planet, eyes of golden tears. All be knowledgeable to go there, knowing the mystery that God is beautiful and wise. He led us to this paradise palace. God is honorable and so good and it makes us extremely happy to do good. Oh, planet, oh eyes of tears.

My United States

United States is a wonderful republic. We love the poor and help them in crisis. We take in other people, give them a chance to live in this great country. God gave us strength; we can do good will to help others. We stand for justice and liberty forever. People come into this country to live, to work, to receive the American way. Thanks to Abraham Lincoln for he was a man of God.

United States is a great country. We had good forefathers who taught the people good examples and build a strong standard to keep America great. We worship God. The blessed Virgin who helps keep our country in good condition and prosperity.

President of the United States shows respect and not disturbed what united should be, honorable above all countries.

In God, we trust. One from many Gods. God watch out for bad presidents. We will be happy in knowing that the United States is a government of the people, by the people, and for the people, so help us God.

Music Brings Out the Love in Me

Music! Music! Bring out the love in me, music bring out the light that lights my soul, the love in me. God gives me a song of poetry, so dainty, so secret, it stains my heart with such a loving flame of desire, so burning into making me a pure angel.

Sing like angels sing spread my wings and fly away in a fairy world. Dance the tango and sweet dream never stop. Make me poetry and sway me to the moon. Let me climb the stairs of Heaven. Let me greet the old moon, laughing at the universe. When holding me so close to my chest and never stop loving your units of greatness only man can stand. I felt when I met you I really was born to be man. I never loved until now, now my soul found desire only you can give me. Then now one can bring me happiness, only love me baby. You are mine, body and soul forever. You are the girl who makes me feel alive and flying in our love. You are my roses, only you will I surrender to.

Last Live Was Frame Via La France

My name is Carol Verillas. I first lived in France in a past life. I do not know where or when, that is what an angel told me in a dream. I lived life and my name was Carol. The angel told me my last name. The name was Messangel. She did not tell me my first. I had a son, Messangel, only worked a conductor of music in a tall building in Paris. The next day I found out I had a son name Messangel, and he was a music conductor in France. I thought to live it alone only hurt people.

All I remember was my death bed in France where I was dying. After that I know nothing else. And now I live in the United States and my name is Carol Verillas. I am a working girl and take care of my old father whom I adore and honor. Strange things to the unknown and of France that life is a mystery. Knowing we get our of life none world enter another light gestation.

A Mother's Love for Her Lisa

Oh! Lisa baby in my arms, I love you so. You're precious, sweet smelling, and fresh breath to me. I love you so much and pray to God for your existence. I never want to lose you. My heart will be terribly sad and lonely if I can't see you. You are the sweetest thing I ever had.

May God give you health and you are lovely, I can't believe it. I wish you the best in life and I'll love you forever. You are my angel of sweetness and kindness, a gift from God.

Lisa love me, too. I hope your life is full of love and happiness. May your spirit live forever. My heart is full of love for my daughter. Bless you when you grow older, let no one hurt you and may God give you protection in any life you live. God created you; He created His masterpiece because I love you until the end of time. I respect your body, love your fingertips, soul, and heart through your pink toes.

Lisa! Lisa! It's written in the sky of Heaven that your mother really loved you. Time will vanish, but my love will last beyond the end of time.

Inside the Stairs

Twinkle, twinkle little stars, your silvery texture, so bright from Earth. I wonder of a star ship that I can see. What's in your starship? Inside you will sparkle like a diamond, cross of both beauty eyes will behold! It's diamonds on the light, walls and where the angels sleep. And your beautiful gold with enormous curtains on the wilderness smell so clean like a pure lemon from the earth. It looks like a silvery dust. Stardust meets do more than girl light to the earth in the dark. I like the angels to bring me on the silvery big star. Let me see the inside of a starship. God made everything distance and privacy after all they don't bother us on Earth.

We should respect other people's property and listen to the rules of planets. We don't want men from space to think we are jealous. We should keep peace with peacemaker too.

When you are far away from another, you should be kind to their beliefs. God bless you and protect other planets and heavenly stairs for they hold up foundation. Emener you can't possess the earth and universe. That belongs to God. The Heaven blesses us with peace.

Little Girl Who Saw Real Saints
under the Tabernacle of the Church

Nancy Edith saw a saint when she went to church. She saw it, Frances Xavier Cabrino, she was under the tabernacle of the church.

Nancy was so impressed to give prayer to this beautiful saint of God. She looked alive, eyes were open, and she was looking up to the sky. The nun had soft brown eyes, a lovely face a true virgin of good, good deed, and good thoughts.

Nancy was happy her aunt took her to New York; she never forgets the nun's face of kindness. I went to New York again to see the saint again. The law authorities moved her out of the church to protect the saint. Someone evil wanted to steal the body, wanted to find out God's secret.

I will always remember the saint. She was good loving and worthy to be a saint. I hope whatever the church did, they wanted to keep such a treasure safe. God must have a safe place where He knows where she is. Saint Francis prays for this world. It's not a safe place to be born.

Glamorous Lady of Spain

Lady you are the white body of a sign of climbing poetry. You're in a world of beauty, in touch with love. Thoughts enter your peaceful mind of wonderful partners. Life can capture your sweetness and honesty. You are a quiet girl full of dreams and desire. You had to be born to help others. Rest and dream of angel love.

Sweetness and goodness is what you bring to me and I appreciate your honesty and your terrific mind.

You dance and sing and act like a good girl should. Sweet lady I love you, our spirit and desirable gentle touch, you have inspired me to do good. By my love and inspire your life by being truthfully to kingdom come.

I love you with my soul, seeing in your eyes deep love. Eyes of good fortune and luck. Man never see your heart in pure gold.

Loving you is all my thoughts, desire, and prayers, my lady. Sweet glamorous lady of Spain, be at my dreams, stay wonderful and loving as you are.

Rhymestone Shoes

Tap, tap away rhyme stone shoes. There I go again tapping my rhyme stone shoes, going get happy and tap the blue days away. Music beats in my heart, my heart is on fire, happy lady I am. My soul is exhausted with love and my shoes never want to stop dancing. I am in the mood, I am devoted to you baby. Every time I see you, I grow more in love with you.

Whenever dancing in the ballroom lights are love. I can crush you close to me, you give me tenderness, more than I hope for and dream of and die for. I live for dreaming of a fantastic love and life with you giving me luck and I will swing to where we really can go dancing. Oh pretty baby never stop me from loving you.

I am on the top of the world and want my baby to be on top of the world with me. On my way to romance and silvery screen and maybe a new house with a picket fence.

Veil of Day Pink

The veil is day pink. It's smooth thin in summer and spring. It's in my bedroom, with flowing curtains and pink flowers.

Romance is my signature to give life a meaning. Then my love kiss my eyes of whipped blues. You kiss my heart and bless my soul and give me a kiss on my hands. Your hands are cold, but there is a breath of sweetness coming from you. When you kissed my mouth, I enjoyed it in extreme passionate beating of my heart content. You're in my life, in my dreams, in my mind. I am lost in your arms. Never to let you out of my existence. You are flaming desire; I cannot put out the fire. You are a prince who rings the bell of eternal love and mystery.

God Bless America

God Bless America! Hang up your flags, Red, White and Blue. Hang high till the holdings climb up and up.

Drums are beating; music is flowing like a blue lagoon. People are watching a parade sitting down by the curb. Children are eating ice cream and they enjoy it. Soldiers march with their heads high in the air, children watching and enjoying the sound of songs. These are giving people change to enjoy the festival. Beautiful girls making in the parade. Oh American girls, you stand for America, you are our future of hope and peace.

Love your country, obey its laws, teach children to love not to hate. Teach our children to help others and love everyone in the world.

Our United States helps us but has the heart to help others who are suffering from wars. Our children all over the nation should find peace and all children should help and grow up to be peacemaker. In the future our children fell love to me another and let love and peace start a better world.

I Dream of Another Planet Called Joyful

I dreamt one night I was in another planet called Joyful. I was beautiful and everyone was happy and enjoying their lives. I met a man name Lowis State. He asked me if I was lost and needed help. I said no! I just found myself, then here and it was at home. It was like an estates beautiful room, more beautiful than Earth. Lowis said he looked at our planet and saw a lot of children and adults without food. I told him we had supermarkets and could not find certain items on Earth. It's too high like Africa and people die from starvation. Other countries help but the earth needs help. I told Lowis I was Mildred Evans and had to be careful how I control money. Don't you worry, Evans, I will help the earth, but don't want them to know of my planet. Earth is not a safe country to deal with. I will drop my aircraft, dozens of items in Africa that will help the people tremendously. The nation I did not see Joyful again. The man Lowis helped the people of Africa and I never saw Joyful again. I think a kind soul managed to do good. We should leave other planets in peace. The universe is big and who knows all of its mystery.

A Dear Father a Kind Soul of a Man

My dearest father was born in 1800. He was a wonderful man. His family was poor; he couldn't eat nothing but hard bread. His mother worked hard, washing clothes by hand. Father went to a place in Florence, Italy, to find a job. There was no work in Genoa, Italy. He died in Florence. There was a war, and he was killed in that war. Mother was so poor, she cried herself to sleep every night.

My father came to America and became a citizen of the United York City as a second cook. He saved his money and worked hard and when he got his first paycheck, he bought a nice steak. He was truly grateful he came to America. He was single until he was 38 and then found my mother in New Jersey and married her. He also had two children. He never forgot his mother and sent her money so she wouldn't be so skinny. It's good to help your mother, a beautiful woman who died at 95. In this country most parents when they get old children then put them in a home. I took care of my father in my home. He worked hard all his life and any daughter should love and take care of her father! Bless the parents!

Face of a Loving God Who Hurts Deeply

God is a loving God who made the world, the animals, and people. When we hurt him by sinning, Jesus runs down his white face. God gave us life and gave us His Commandments! Life will be good to them. We must love ourselves and love others. We must not lie or cheat or kill another person or rob or take God's name in vain.

God is giving himself in the holy Eucharist; He gave us the right to be born. God gave us parents. Honor thy father and mother. He gave us commandments for the love of the church. Gave us penance so we could go to Heaven. He gave the people the holy sacrament like matrimony. He gave us the holy obligations of the church all saints. He gave us the gift of life and the power to get to Heaven. Whatever did we give God? Only sorrow, pain, suffering, thy ever hang His Son Jesus on the cross.

A man who spoke of love and loving others we will be rewarded if we listen and love God. Heaven is very clean, it's beautiful. Sky is pure blue the sun is brighter and life in Heaven will make man very happy. You will honor goodness and kindness; you will know what really love is. Every step you take you enjoy education. Education and life came from God. Poetry will stand out in Heaven and maybe you will understand life. Poetry is a gift and God can give beside all men.

A Portrait of Mary Queen of the Angels

Oh! Blessed Mary queen of the angels. Queen of the angels, you were a good mother, loving St. Joseph and Jesus who loved you deeply. Mary had beautiful eyes that only God can give. She was born clean and not with actual sin. That's why God created baptism. In baptism, our souls are clean. Mary was born without sin. This must be beautiful queen of heaven. Pray for us so we grow up in God's mind. Give us strength to become a better human being. Give us hope, clarity, and to thank God. May God give us a clean thoughtful mind. Bless us with baptism for humility. May all of us be good to others, give them peace. We should feed the hungry and the animals, too. They are made by God, too. Our hearts should listen to Mary, how can you not listen to this queen of Heaven. Whose can't be beat by others. In Heaven she must sparkle like a real diamond. She wears the crown of Heaven. Heaven was in her by her beauty and goodness. Her soul sparkles in Heaven, for she outshines even the saints, when die. I should see her hand and tell them in Heaven, take care of the poor on Earth.

My Aunt Edith

My Aunt Edith was a caring, wonderful person. I love her like I love my mother. She had a husband and nice daughter name Marie. I felt sorry because when I was young, she was sick a lot, it saddened me. She was good to me and took care of me when I was sick, and my blood count went down to 30. I was suffering from iron deficiency. I could not get up from the bed. She came over every day to take care of me, to take me to the bathroom. She cleaned for me and cooked for me. God bless you Aunt Edith. She had a heart of God. It took three months but she was good to a niece like me.

Now she has passed away. I still care about her and hope Heaven fills her with joy and promise and other life because she was so good the first time around.

I'll always remember when I die to meet Aunt Edith and kiss her again. Between Aunt Edith, grandma, my mother, and my father, I was in good hands forever. Don't let me forget I was always in good hands with God.

Dear Saint Bernadette I Pray To You

    Dear Saint Bernadette, I pray to you. Give me hope and a good heart. Make me understand prayers helping people, helping children, helping animals. Make my soul and may thoughts think of others. Let me help the starving children of the world. I wish I was young again, soul, Heaven, animals to take care. I used to take care of animals, but I am not stable to walk good. I hate being old, then a lot of pain in my bones. I can't type because it makes my hands hurt. I can't walk good so I am confined to home.

    Please let me feel better so I can do my purpose and write. Let me pray for others, too. I am sure old men feel pain, too. Teach me to be brave and wonderful, like you always smile even in pain. You are strong and a perfect saint. I wish I could take our pain away, but it was destiny and God will prevail.

    Find in your heart to forgive me for being so weak. I need to think of others whose lives are even worse.

Love Me Till the End of New Life

    Madam, I love your pretty fingertips. Your soul is a moving motion of tranquility. Your eyes and ears are so perfectly fixed on your face. You are an angel of golden wings, like a red robin in atmosphere.

    You are singing like a blue bird of happiness, sweet little bird singing your happy song. Tapping on your window sill, are you Cinderella so far and pretty in yellow?

No, I am not Cinderella, but I know about Cinderella. She works hard and birds know, too, if they work hard, they will have a nice little nest to put their babies in. Cinderella always attracted birds that sang to her in yellow or pink. Cinderella was imagining colors.

Bugs Bunny Don't Eat No Honey for Children

Bugs Bunny don't eat no honey. They love carrots. One day Bugs Bunny put a popsicle in his mouth, and he went out for a day. Bugs Bunny said beautiful morning. Dance in the pond, fresh great grass growing on the ground. He wanted to see Lucy Duck. They went to Friends Park to have their picnic of fried chicken, potato salad, and of course pickles and beautiful round buns.

Bugs Bunny saw Lucy Duck three times a week. Other days he went to work, growing carrots in the backyard. Bugs loved carrots and couldn't live without them. He would make sure Lucy brought some carrots on the picnic. Bunny had a sweet little home with a white picket fence. He was an old soul. He had his nephew come to visit him and bring him carrots; he could not get enough of them. He didn't want to be married, just wanted to be good friends with Lucy Duck. Lucy Duck said if that Bunny don't marry me, I'll start dating Porky Pig. Bunny was hurt but he got over it fast saying, I got good friends. I got my carrots, got my nephew who needs a troublesome duck. I still have plenty of carrots, got my Lucy and still to a stop, he said, I still got my white house with a pretty fence.

My home is so refreshed and clean. That's all, folks.

www.ingramcontent.com/pod-product-compliance
Lightning Source LLC
Chambersburg PA
CBHW032007060426

42449CB00032B/1182